JUMPSTART!
SCIENCE

The *Jumpstart!* books contain 'quick-fire' ideas that could be used as warm-ups and starters as well as possibly extended into lessons. There are more than 50 provocative games and activities for Key Stage 1 or 2 classrooms. Practical, easy-to-do and vastly entertaining, the 'jumpstarts' will appeal to busy teachers in any primary classroom.

Also available in the series:

JUMPSTART!
SCIENCE

GAMES AND ACTIVITIES FOR AGES 5–11

Rosemary Feasey

Routledge
Taylor & Francis Group

LONDON AND NEW YORK

First published 2009
by Routledge
2 Park Square, Milton Park, Abingdon, Oxon, OX14 4RN

Simultaneously published in the USA and Canada
by Routledge
711 Third Avenue, New York, NY 10017

Routledge is an imprint of the Taylor & Francis Group, an informa business

Typeset in Palatino and Scala Sans by FiSH Books, Enfield

British Library Cataloguing in Publication Data
A catalogue record for this book is available from the British Library

Library of Congress Cataloging in Publication Data
Feasey, Rosemary.
Jumpstart! Science : games and activities for ages 5–11 / Rosemary Feasey.
    p. cm. – (Jumpstart!)
1. Science–Study and teaching (Elementary)–Activity programs–Great
Britain. I. Title.
LB1585.5.G7F43 2009
372.35'044–dc22   008040872

ISBN 10: 0-415-48212-7 (pbk)
ISBN 10: 0-203-88036-6 (ebk)

ISBN 13: 978-0-415-48212-7 (pbk)
ISBN 13: 978-0-203-88036-4 (ebk)

Contents

Acknowledgements

I have been blessed with a husband and family who have supported me in my work and taken great pride in what I do. Despite my moments of grumpiness at stressful moments when deadlines loom, they have put up with me.

Throughout my career I have had the privilege of working with teachers from around the world and have never ceased to be amazed by their energy, enthusiasm and generosity in sharing ideas with me. This book is a collection of those ideas, and in particular I would like to thank the many teachers in the north east of England who not only offered activities but also trialled and commented on the games in this book. You are all brilliant, in particular Linda James, a great friend and colleague.

Once again my sincere thanks to Roy and Anne Phipps who, although retired, have taken the time to read and critique this book.

I would like to thank TTS Group for their kind permission to use the photographs in this book.

Dedication
Finally, I would like to dedicate this book to my wonderful family – my husband Steve, my Mum, my sister Melanie, my nieces Katrina, Simone and Collette who are my pride and joy and, finally, to my Auntie Pam whose courage and love is an inspiration to me.

Introduction

Jumpstart! Science games are intended to offer teachers short, fun activities to develop different aspects of science learning. Fun is the key word; the games are meant to engage and motivate children to develop different aspects of their science and, hopefully, will leave children wanting to play the games again and again. . .

WHY PLAY GAMES IN SCIENCE?

Science is a wonderful area of the curriculum which aims to inspire lively minds to make sense of the world around them. We would like children to remember their science as a mixture of awe, challenge, intrigue, fascinating ideas and useful skills as well as fun.

The games and activities in this book are designed to make learning different ideas and skills interesting and easy and to offer opportunities for the necessary repetition and reinforcement that children need to embed ideas and skills. They can be used to:

- develop observation skills;
- introduce new ideas;
- reinforce and consolidate learning;
- teach language;
- develop recall;
- apply knowledge;
- practise skills;

- challenge; and
- develop creativity.

WHEN CAN THE GAMES BE USED?

The simple answer is: 'At any point in a lesson where it is appropriate', for example:

- as a starter;
- as a bridge from one activity to another;
- where new impetus for motivation is perceived by the teacher;
- as a stand-alone activity;
- as part of a plenary;
- as part of booster classes; or
- in science clubs.

USING JUMPSTART! SCIENCE

Whilst the games and activities in *Jumpstart! Science* can be used for a range of purposes, you might find it helpful to consider the following points:

- Allocate a time in most lessons for a *Jumpstart* game, between 5 and 15 minutes.
- Link the games to current science teaching and learning, or revision of previous topics.
- Adapt games to suit the age and ability of your children.
- Use the same game on a regular basis; children love activities that they are familiar with, and will, over time, develop their favourite ones.
- Most of the games are meant to be collaborative, so it is important for children to work in small groups (up to four children) or with their science partners (pairs) to support each other, in sharing and clarifying ideas before responding.

- Many of the games support speaking and listening in science so discussion is an important part of many of the activities.
- Give children time to think and formulate their responses – to draft and redraft before they say something or write something down.

ADAPTING THE GAMES

The aim is to explain the game and suggest how it can be used, but the best use of the material is when the teacher and children decide how to use and change the game to suit themselves. Once you are familiar with a game or activity you might adapt it so that it can be used with:

- the whole class;
- small groups;
- science partners; and
- different science topics.

REVISION SESSIONS

All ideas in this book will provide interesting ways for children to revise their science, particularly for tests.

TEACHING AND LEARNING ASSISTANTS (TAs/LAs)

Don't forget to give TAs and LAs access to this book so that they understand the activities that you have chosen to use. Equally important is for them to use and, where appropriate, adapt the material for the children they support in science.

SCIENCE CLUBS

The material in *Jumpstart! Science* is excellent for children attending science clubs.

SCIENCE ACTIVITY TABLE

Children of all ages enjoy repeating favourite activities, so when children have played a game or tried out an activity, place the material on the classroom science activity table so that they can access it at their leisure.

LEARNING STYLE SYMBOLS

Alongside each activity you will find one of the following symbols which indicates the learning styles applied during that activity or game.

Visual   Auditory   Cognitive   Kinaesthetic

CHAPTER 1

Jumpstarting science questioning

The activities in this chapter focus on developing children's ability to ask and answer questions. Effective questioning is central to science and being able to ask and answer a range of questions is an aspect of science that the teacher needs to plan into science sessions on a regular basis. This chapter begins with an activity in which children are introduced to the use of question stem cards. These are then used in a range of different activities throughout this book.

QUESTIONS

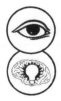

Questioning

Resources
Question stem cards *or*
Question fans

What if...?

How can...?

Figure 1 Question stem cards

This activity has been chosen to be the first in the book because the set of question cards or (if you prefer a question fan) that is required can be used in a range of other games and activities throughout this book. It is worth making this set of cards or the fan for your class; they will be used again and again.

- The teacher could create the question stems for the interactive whiteboard and introduce this activity as a whole-class session.
- To make the cards use Word to create call-out shapes with different question stems in each one. Print them out, laminate and cut out the shapes. Include question stems such as:

Why?	Which?	Where?	Did?	Could?
Can?	How?	How does?	What if?	
Should?	When?	Will?	Who?	Does?

It is useful to make a set of cards for each group in the class. Make sure you print the call-outs on a different-colour paper so that if the cards get mixed up they can be sorted easily, and place in small plastic wallets to keep them together.
- Each group keeps its set of cards on their table ensuring that the question stem cards are always available for science lessons and other subject areas across the curriculum. If you prefer to make the science fan, it is quite simple and is similar to a numeracy number fan but with question stems printed or written on each segment.
- To use the question stem cards, children place all of the question stems face up on the table and use them to ask different questions about a topic – for example, space – or an object such as an animal skull.
- When they have used a question stem they should turn the card over so that it cannot be used again. This challenges the children to use different questions stems.

- Some question stems might be more problematic than others and require the teacher to intervene and model examples of questions – for example, Could it. . .? and Would it. . .? questions.
- The number of question stem cards that the children are given could be varied according to the ability of the children.
- When children are asking questions relating to a specific topic – for example, plant growth – give them key scientific vocabulary that they need to use when asking their questions.
- One member of the group scribes the questions that the children ask so that they have a record of them. Where children have limited written skills the teacher or teaching assistant could scribe for them.
- Once they have finished asking their questions children should find ways of answering them.
- If using the question fans, children use the questions working from one end of the fan to the other.

WHAT'S IN HERE?

Skills development
Questioning
Use and apply knowledge and understanding
Analysis

Resources
Surprise box or a surprise bag
Science items for the box or bag
Science question stem cards (see page 1)

Children really enjoy the challenge of this activity where they have to work out what is in the surprise box or surprise bag. Teachers who use this activity find that children get very excited if the surprise box is made to look special – for example, by covering it with

3

sparkly wrapping paper or using pictures on each face of the box. Once used, children delight in using it again and again, as well as taking charge of the activity and creating their own surprise boxes or bags to use in their own class or with younger children.

- To start, show the children the surprise box or bag and tell them that there is something very special or interesting in the box – for example, a prism, animal skull, slimy substance or clockwork toy. Explain that if they want to find out what it is they must ask really good questions. You might, for example, say that they can only ask ten questions and they must listen to the other questions and the answers to help them solve the mystery of what is in the box.
- Use the question stem cards from the first activity on page 2, which could be stuck on to the faces of the box as cues for the children, or the children could use their question stem card sets.
- There are many things that could be placed in the box or bag, from a feather to a fossil. This activity could be used in many different ways – for example:
  - as a regular activity to develop children's questioning skills;
  - as a starting point for science discussion; or
  - as a starting point for a topic.
- Alternatively, the surprise box could be used as a starting point for a fair test investigation. For example, with young children, place a teddy bear in the box with a pair of broken sunglasses and a sun hat. If children work out that teddy is in the box, then ask children where they think teddy is going and what is his problem, and ask them to suggest how they might solve it. The aim would be for children to design and test a new pair of sunglasses for teddy.
- For older children you could put a broken torch

inside that would lead to children designing and making a working torch.

PREDATORS AND PREY

Questioning
Use and apply knowledge and understanding

Resources
List of questions
Team mascot, e.g. predators – soft toy owl; prey – soft toy mouse

This is a great activity for reinforcing and revising vocabulary and subject knowledge from the current or previous topics. It could also be used to introduce new vocabulary at the beginning of a lesson. Before starting this activity the teacher needs to have created a bank of questions relating to the areas the teacher wants to revise.

- Divide the class into two groups. They could be given any name that they wish, but here the suggestion is 'predators' and 'prey'. Children really like it if they can have a team mascot – for example, a soft toy owl (predator) and a mouse (prey).
- The teacher asks the children questions, each team taking it in turns to answer, and points are awarded for correct responses. If one team is unable to answer a question it can be 'thrown open' to the other team, and if they provide a correct answer they win half the original points.
- This activity works even better if children create their own question bank, or a question bank for a younger class to use. Developing their own questions and checking the answers is an excellent revision exercise and younger year groups will enjoy playing the game using the questions children from another class have produced.

SINK THE BOAT

Questioning
Scientific vocabulary

Resources
Question stem cards
Scientific objects
Masses, washers or stones
Plastic container, e.g. margarine or ice-cream container
Plastic aquarium

Children really enjoy the excitement of this game, which challenges them to think carefully about the questions they are asking and the clues in the answers that are given.

- A familiar scientific object is placed in a box or bag and children are challenged to find out what the object is using their question stems (see page 2).
- Use objects that the children need to become familiar with, e.g. pipette, Newton meter, crocodile clip.
- To provide an added challenge and a fun element to this activity, every time a question is asked, place a plastic mass, washer or stone in a plastic container in a plastic aquarium of water. The children have to work out what is in the box or bag before the container sinks. Children love this challenge and the suspense is tangible as the container gradually sinks lower into the water.
- Do allow the children to organize this activity so that someone chooses the object, another child is in charge of the boat and a different child chooses someone to ask a question.
- Children find this activity challenging and the teacher might need to intervene to remind children to pay attention if they repeat questions that have already been asked or to remind them of the clues in answers that have been given.

- This game can be played with word cards. One child picks a science word card and the children have to work out, through their questions, what word is on the card. This can be used as a science revision activity at the end of topics or to develop children's scientific language during a topic.

HOT SEATING

Questioning
Speaking and listening
Use and apply knowledge and understanding

Resources
None required

This activity is great as a starter activity or as an end to a lesson.

- Prepare a list of five to nine words your class has recently learned.
- Divide the class into two teams. One person from each team moves to a 'special chair' at the front of the room and faces the class. This person is now in the hot seat. The chairs could be decorated with science words or symbols to make them more special.
- Write a scientific word on the board, making sure the players in the 'hot seats' can't see it. After you say 'Go!' the members of each team give clues to their person in the 'hot seat' but they must not say the word itself and they cannot give spelling clues. They can, however, provide clues such as the following for the word 'Friction': 'Cars need this so that they do not skid.' The team whose 'hot seat' player first says the word wins a point.
- After the first round the two players in the 'hot seats' then swap seats with another member of

their respective teams. The game continues and the team with the most points at the end is the winner.

• This does not have to be set up as a competitive game; it could be arranged so that there is just one person in the hot seat and the other children try to elicit the word from the person in the hot seat.

WHAT'S THE QUESTION?

Questioning
Use and apply knowledge and understanding

Resources
None required

This is a very challenging activity and makes a range of demands on children's language in science. Instead of asking children a question for them to answer, this activity gives the children the answer and asks them to work out what the question was.

• An example would be giving children the answer, such as 'conductor'. The children are challenged to work backwards and decide what the original question might be that would result in 'conductor' as the answer, e.g 'What do we call a person on a bus who collects fares?

• When playing this game with children, don't be afraid to challenge their responses, for example:

Teacher:	The answer is 'conductor'. What is the question?
Child:	The question is, What lets electricity through?
Teacher:	The answer to that could be metal.
Child:	Oh, yeah.
Teacher:	Who can change that question so that it gives the answer 'conductor'?

This is an excellent activity to use towards the end of a science topic to help children revise their understanding.

This activity could be used at the beginning of each lesson. Place a set of words on the whiteboard for children to create the question, then ask them to write their questions on their mini whiteboards. The teacher can ask children to hold up their mini whiteboards. This enables the teacher to view all of the responses around the classroom at once.

The more frequently the children engage in this activity the more precise they will become with their questions.

Allow children to work in pairs or in small groups. This allows children to share ideas, challenge each other and draft and redraft their questions.

CHAPTER 2

Jumpstarting science vocabulary

The focus of the activities in this chapter is scientific vocabulary. Children really enjoy using exciting new words, and science has a rich and interesting technical vocabulary; one which children need to learn, otherwise their ability to think, speak and write in science will be limited. In order for children to become fluent in any language they need to see, hear, speak and write the words on a regular basis. Science has its own special language that needs to be used constantly.

To support children in learning scientific vocabulary, set aside five to ten minutes every lesson to engage children in one or more of the games or activities in this chapter.

SCIENCE ALPHABET

Vocabulary
Use and apply knowledge and understanding

Resources
None required

This is an excellent activity that can be used in a variety of ways. Children create their own science alphabet, beginning at A and ending with Z, but they must use scientific vocabulary and words must be spelled correctly if written down.

In this activity children could create a science alphabet related to a particular area of science – for example, an animal alphabet or a general science alphabet, which could contain scientific words from different areas of science.

This could be used as an activity where a group of children work together to create their alphabet, perhaps as a poster. Allow children to research their words and check the spellings.

Alternatively, this could be played as a whole-class game where one child offers a scientific word beginning with A and the next person thinks of a word for B and so on. If someone is unable to think of a word they have to sit out and the class continues from that word. The last person remaining is the winner of the game, or the child that can't answer could be given an item to hold and then passes the item to the next child who can't answer, where upon the first child can be re-enter the game.

To add a little fun to the game the teacher could give the children a letter of the alphabet to start the game, for example, F, or the teacher could say, 'Work backwards from Z'.

PREFIXES AND SUFFIXES

Scientific vocabulary
Use and apply knowledge and understanding

Resources
Flashcards

Developing children's understanding and use of scientific vocabulary is supported when children learn that we can understand what some words mean if we know about prefixes and suffixes.

- This activity requires the teacher to create pairs of cards. One card has a prefix or suffix and the other has its meaning.
- To play the game children shuffle the cards, place them face down and then take turns to turn one card face up and then another, to see if they have the pair.
- They repeat this until they have collected all the pairs. The person with the most pairs wins the game.
- The cards can also be used as flashcards where the teacher or the children show the flashcard and someone explains what the prefix means and gives an example of a word.

Table 1 Prefixes and suffixes in science

Prefix or suffix	Word examples
Photo- means light	photograph photosynthesis
Bio- means life	biology biodegradable
Anti- means against	antibacterial antimalarial
Dis- and un- mean not or opposite	disappear
Bi- means two	biceps bicycle biology

Table 1 Prefixes and suffixes in science (continued)

Prefix or suffix	Word examples
Micro- means small	microscope microscopic microchip micro-organism
Tri- means three	triceratops tripod tricycle
-able means able to	dissolvable
-ible means to be reversed	reversible
-ous means full of	gaseous luminous

WORD ASSOCIATIONS

Scientific vocabulary
Use and apply knowledge and understanding
Speaking and listening

Resources
Any of the following:
List of scientific vocabulary
List of science-related places, e.g. rainforest
List of scientists, inventions, discoveries

This is a game that can be used as a starter, part of a plenary or as a break between one part of a science lesson and another.

- The teacher needs a list of words that can be used as a starting point, or one of the children can begin the game with a word of their choice. Once the first word has been offered to the class the children take turns to offer a word that has some association, for example:

Starter word   battery

Associated words   circuit > switch > wire > conductor > thermal > heat > temperature > thermometer > measure > Newton meter

- You will notice that in the list of 'Associated Words' the progression is from words associated with electricity, then heat through to measurement. The words do not have to link to the original word but they do have to link to the last word offered.
- The aim of the game is to keep making associations until there is a break when someone cannot suggest an association or does not make one within, say, 30 seconds. Where children lack confidence or need support, allow them to work in pairs and give the pair time to think of a response.
- It is a quick game that certainly generates excitement, especially when the teacher keeps a record of how many associations children make in a session, and each time the children play this game they try to beat their previous score.

RUN ROUND QUIZ

Scientific vocabulary
Use and apply knowledge and understanding

Resources
Laminated flash cards
School hall or playground

This is a simple but effective game that helps children to develop their understanding of scientific terms and concepts. It requires space for children to move around, so ideally it should be played in the hall or in the playground.

- The words should be related to the science topic children are currently working on or a topic that is being revised. There are a number of websites that offer free science vocabulary flash cards – for example, http://www.sheffield.gov.uk/education/information-for-schools/good-practice/curriculum/science/primary/vocabulary/flash-cards
- The children place the flash cards face up on the hall floor or outside on the playground, which is great if it is a dry, but not if it isn't!
- Divide the children into two or more teams.
- The teacher then chooses a word and begins to describe this word without using the word itself – for example, 'They are hard, they are bones and they protect our heart and lungs.' When the children think that they know the word they run for the correct word. The first team to give the word to the teacher gets a point. If the children are working in teams they can take it in turns to run for the answer. When using words for this game do not forget to use words related to scientific enquiry such as conclusion, analyse, graph, pattern, trend, variable, fair, table, measure, plan, observe, predict.

FOLLOW ME CARDS

Scientific vocabulary
Use and apply knowledge and understanding

Resources
'Follow me' cards are used across the curriculum areas. They are great fun and children enjoy using them. They are best used with small groups or pairs.

- There are two sets of cards; the first set contains the words, the second has the word definitions. Children need to follow the word with a card that shows the correct definition.
- Children can play this as a game where each child holds a number of cards in their hand and the child who gets rid of his or her cards first wins.
- Alternatively, children could take it in turns to take a card from the pile in the middle of their table to see if it matches the card on top of the discarded pile. If it does then that child can take the pair of cards. The child who has the most pairs of cards at the end of the game is the winner.
- Different groups could play different follow me card games, but remember to find some way of marking the cards so that, at a quick glance, the teacher or the children can tell if a card has been put in the wrong pack. Laminating the cards ensures that the cards can be used again and again. Make sure that the children place them into the plastic wallet when they have finished.
- Put the cards out on a science activity table so that children can use them when they have some spare time.

SINGING SCIENTIFIC WORDS

Scientific vocabulary

Resources
None required

This is a fun activity that children of all ages love to do. It is very simple but should be part of regular, sustained strategies, supporting children learning scientific vocabulary. As part of introducing a new word in science, particularly a key word, ask children to do the following:

- Listen to the word.
- Say the word.
- Read the word.
- Look at the spelling of the word.
- Note any key features, e.g. shape, parts.
- Decide how many syllables the word has.
- Clap the rhythm of the word.
- Say the word again.
- Whisper the word.
- Shout the word.
- Sing the word in a particular style, e.g. opera, rap.
- Say the word so that it sounds like the meaning of the word – for example, the word 'elastic' would sound like a piece of elastic being stretched and then snapping back ('eee-laaast-ick').

Each time children engage with the word it is helping them to become familiar with the sound of the word, its syllables and its spelling.

Children will enjoy returning to words they already know as well as singing new words.

SIGNING SCIENTIFIC WORDS

Scientific vocabulary
Use and apply knowledge and understanding

Resources
None required

This is a variation of the previous activity, 'Singing Scientific Words'. Explain to children that they are going to create new signs for words that they already know in science, and each time they learn a new word, ask children to create a sign for it and share it with their science partner and with the rest of the class.

- Explain to the children that the sign has to show the meaning of the word; easy examples are 'push' and 'pull'.
- Children are very imaginative. When a class of children was asked to create a sign for the word 'elastic' they used their hands to show stretching something and snapping back – a catapult being fired – and some children even pulled at their trouser or skirt waistband.
- Encourage children to use the hand signs to remind them of words. Some children have been noticed in tests signing to themselves to help them remember their science.
- Allow children to take photographs of each other signing and create a photographic signing album.

SCIENCE WHISPERS

Scientific vocabulary
Speaking and listening

Resources
None required

This activity is an old favourite and is based on the game Chinese Whispers. It is very useful for developing children's ability in speaking, listening and memory in science. It is a short, fun activity where one or two children choose one of the following to send as a whispered message around the class:

- a scientific word;
- phrase;
- definition of a scientific word;
- science fact;
- piece of science information; or
- name of a scientist, discovery or invention.

- The children write the message on a piece of paper or an individual whiteboard, which is kept secret from everyone else until the end.
- The message is whispered to the next child, who then whispers it to the next and so on, until it has been passed round all of the children in the class.
- The last person to receive the message has to tell the class what they heard and this is compared to the original message that was written down as evidence of what was said at the beginning.
- To add an extra dimension everyone could be given a class point if they manage to send the message round the class unchanged.

SCIENCE CALLIGRAMS

Scientific vocabulary
Use and apply knowledge and understanding

Resources
None required

The word 'calligrams' means beautiful writing. Today we can use word art to create a calligram, where the way the words are written suggests what the word means, for example:

Figure 2 Science calligrams

- In science we can use calligrams to help children learn how to spell words and to develop their understanding of the meaning of the word. This approach is particularly useful when children are learning about materials and their properties.
- When children are learning a new word, ask them to create a calligram using the word. Challenge the children to make sure that when the word is read by someone else the meaning of the word can be seen in the calligram.
- There are many words that can be easily used for science calligrams, for example:

transparent	opaque	translucent	friable
porous	graph	axis	friction
gravity	solid	gas	liquid

- Display science calligrams around the classroom or create a class book of science calligrams.

UNSCRAMBLE THE SCIENCE WORDS

Scientific vocabulary

Resources
None required

This is a quick, easy game that can be played during those few minutes spent waiting for the class to settle at the beginning of a lesson or as children wait for everyone to finish clearing up after a practical activity.

- Place a set of words on a board, flip chart or interactive whiteboard.
- Challenge the children to unscramble the words; you might like to give them a time period – for example, using a sand timer or a piece of music.
- Words can be differentiated according to the ability

of the children, with more able children being given a different set of words that extends their scientific vocabulary beyond the basic vocabulary for the topic area.

- For those children who have difficulty with spellings you could provide the answers at the side of the board or allow them to use their personal science dictionaries or a word mat. Word mats can be downloaded from http://www.sheffield.gov.uk/education/information-for-schools/good-practice/curriculum/science/primary/vocabulary/key-stage-2/year-4-word-mats

SCIENCE CHARADES

Use and apply knowledge and understanding
Scientific vocabulary

Resources
Science word cards

This game is the same as the party game charades, but usually the class is only asked to guess one word, not a phrase.

- Make sure that the words are within the experience of the children and include proper nouns such as famous scientists, planets or constellations.
- One person acts out a word and the rest of the class guess the word or phrase.
- The class could be divided into teams and scores could be kept on the success of the individual teams to guess their word.
- This is a great game to play on a daily basis over a week. It allows most children in the class to be the person miming the charade and for teams to accrue lots of points, which children love to do.

In order to play this game children will need to learn some basic signals, such as:

Correct guess	point to their nose and the person making the correct guess
Sounds like	cup one hand behind an ear
Long word	pretend to stretch a piece of elastic
Short word	move two hands together
Name of a person	tap the top of head
Close, keep guessing!	wave hands about
Not close	pretend to shiver
Start again	move hand in a wide sweep in front of the body

SCIENCE TABOO

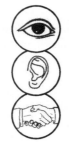

Scientific vocabulary
Speaking and listening

Resources
Taboo cards – draw, speak, mime
Buzzer
Timer

This is a fun game for children that can be played as a whole class or in teams and is designed to develop and extend children's scientific language.

- One person (the player) from each team goes to the front of the class and is given a card with a scientific word on it. The player has to try to explain the word on the card without using the word itself. If their team guesses the word within the allocated time they win a point. If they do not, then it is thrown open to the other group. If the 'player' inadvertently uses the word on the card then the teacher shouts 'Taboo' and the other team wins a point.

- The team that guesses the correct word wins the point.
- A variation of this game is for the player to choose how to describe the word using taboo cards say, 'Draw', 'Mime' or 'Words'.

SCIENCE ACROSTICS

Scientific vocabulary
Speaking and listening
Use and apply knowledge and understanding

Resources
Word bags
Science word cards

This is a tried and tested favourite that children enjoy and that can be carried out in pairs or small groups, where children use the letters in a science word to begin the line of a poem and all of the lines should relate to the word, for example:

Silently
Twinkling
Anonymously
Radiating

- Children are given, or choose, a scientific word and have to make an acrostic using the letters of the word. Remind children how to produce acrostics by creating an acrostic with the whole class.
- It is much more fun if children are given a word bag in which a range of scientific words are placed and they take pot luck with regard to which word they pull out of the bag.

- Explain to children that they should draft and redraft their acrostic using their mini whiteboards, discussing with their partner the best words to place in the acrostic. Children could use a different, coloured pen for the initial letter of each row.
- An important aspect of science word ladders is that the children should use scientific vocabulary, and knowledge and understanding when creating them, as in the following examples:

Busy	**C**ircle
Energetic	**I**nsulator
Environmentally friendly	**R**eed switch
	Cell
	Unipolar
	Insulator
	Terminal

30 SECONDS GAME

Scientific vocabulary

Resources
None required

This is another simple yet effective game which encourages children to apply their scientific knowledge and understanding. In this activity children work with their science partners and are shown a word – for example, 'flexible'. Then children have a set time, say 30 seconds, to take turns and tell each other objects that have the property of flexibility – for example, body, plastic ruler, pipe cleaner. Each time one of the partners names something they keep a tally score on their mini whiteboard. At the end of the 30 seconds everyone in the class holds up their mini whiteboard and science partners with the highest tally score are the winners.

I AM GOING ON A SCIENCE TRIP

Scientific vocabulary
Memory

Resources
None required

There are many old favourite games that children know and are great to use in science lessons. This game is based on games where children have to remember and add to a list of items – for example, 'Today I went shopping and I bought . . .', or, ' I am going camping and I will take . . .'.

- In this version the teacher or a child starts the game by saying 'Today we are going to do science. We will need a . . .', and then chooses a piece of science equipment or resource. This is passed on to the next person who repeats what has just been said and adds another piece of science equipment.
- The list continues to be added to but if someone forgets any of the list, they must sit down, and only those left standing can continue the game.
- The winner is the person who is left standing, and that person is allowed to start the game the next time it is played.
- You could add variety to this game and challenge children to beat their own target – for example, how many people can add to the list before the chain is broken? If in one game 14 children manage to add to the list before the chain is broken, then the teacher records that number and the next time the game is played the children have to try to beat the target of 14.
- You could also vary the game by stipulating a topic, e.g. electricity.
- Alternatively you could use this game to help children or a small group plan a fair test investigation, e.g. we are going to do an investigation on dissolving sugars, we will need . . .

CHAPTER 3
Jumpstarting science observation

In science, observation is either an activity where children use all or some of their five senses to make sense of their environment and scientific phenomena or it is related to measuring and recording scientific data.

Observation games and activities are also very important for developing children's visual memory. For some children it is one of their preferred ways of learning; for others it is something that is useful to develop.

The activities in this chapter have been chosen to develop both aspects of observation in science.

KIM'S GAME

Observation
Use and apply knowledge and understanding
Science spelling

Resources
Familiar science equipment, e.g. Newton meter, pipette, spirit thermometer
Sheets of A3 paper

Kim's Game is a game that has been played for over 100 years. It focuses on observation and developing children's capacity to make observations and remember details. This is a great game when adapted to be played in science, very easy to set up and great fun.

- Children really enjoy this game; it tests their memory and they find it quite challenging. This game is simple to organize and is a science version of Kim's Game where the players have to remember a set of objects before they are covered or taken away. In this version the teacher places 10–15 items of science equipment that children have used, either in their recent or previous topics, on a large sheet of paper or a tray, but behind something, so that the class cannot see the objects.
- The children are divided into groups of four to six and each child is allocated a number from 1 to however many are in each group. When the covered objects are revealed the teacher calls out one of the numbers – for example, the number 3, and all those children with that number go over to the table. They are given around 15 seconds to memorize as many objects as they can and their positions. Remember to allow only the children whose number has been called to see the objects, not the rest of the class.
- When each child returns to their group they draw and label as many objects as they can remember on a large sheet of paper and, for a challenge, the correct position in relation to other objects. As they are doing this the teacher calls out another number and repeats the process.
- When all the children have had sufficient visits to the table, the teacher stops the game and helps the children to score their efforts. Depending on the ability of the children this could include giving points, for example:
  - one point for the correct object
  - one point for the correct name

- one point for the correct spelling
- one point for the correct position.
- You could try this game with different objects depending on the science topic being taught. For example, you could use equipment relating to scientific enquiry such as pipettes, stop watches and capacity containers, or items relating to topics, such as Materials, such as a metal ruler, wooden spoon, plastic plate, clay brick, polystyrene cup and wool scarf.
- An alternative is to place items on a tray and show them to each group telling the children that they must remember what is on the tray. The tray is then covered with a cloth and the children work in pairs to write down how many pieces of equipment they can name and spell correctly.
- Make sure that they focus on the spelling, since this activity is designed to support children in learning scientific vocabulary. Before you start, check that you know the correct name and spelling of each item.

ODD ONE OUT

Observation
Speaking and listening

Resources
Any of the following:
Pictures
Objects
Words

This is an activity that generates lively discussions amongst groups of children. The idea is that the teacher places three or more 'science' objects in front of children, but one of the objects is the odd one out.

- The children have to decide which one it is. They cannot just guess which one, they have to explain what the others have in common and why the object they have chosen is the odd one out.
- The teacher can vary the challenge in this activity by increasing the number of things put in front of the children or the difficulty of the concept, or by choosing items of which more than one could be the odd one.
- You might decide to place objects, pictures or words in front of children, depending on their age and ability. For example:
  - pictures of a spider, cockroach, ladybird, ant, dragonfly (odd one out is the spider; it has eight legs);
  - pictures of a ladybird, worm, spider, snail (odd one out is the snail; gardeners like the other insects; snails eat plants);
  - objects – cork, aluminium foil, plastic ruler, twig (aluminium foil is the odd one out because it conducts electricity; the other materials are insulators);
  - words – condensation, evaporation, dissolve, ice, distill, pollinate (pollinate is the odd one out because all of the others are about water; pollination is about plants).

THE SCIENCE VILLAGE

Observation
Scientific vocabulary

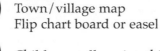

Resources
Town / village map
Flip chart board or easel

Children really enjoy this activity and once they have played it they usually ask to play it over and over again. It helps children to develop their ability and personal strategies for memorizing information and learning scientific terms and spellings.

- This activity requires a simple map of a town or village with features such as roads, railway stations, parks, buildings etc. to be created. Each of the features should be labelled using a scientific term that could be related to the topic that the children are learning, or a revision area, as in Figure 3.
- The map is placed on a flip chart board or easel where the whole class cannot see it. The class is split into groups of four to five children and each child is given a number from 1 to 5. The groups have marker pens and a large sheet of paper.
- The aim of the activity is for each group to redraw the science village exactly.
- When the game is played the teacher calls out a number and the person with that number from each group goes up to the picture, memorizes part of it, including positions, and then returns to their group and draws what they have remembered on the paper at their own table. The teacher then calls a different number, and different children go up. The process is repeated until the teacher says 'stop'.
- Groups can be awarded points for how many of the features they have correctly drawn on their map in the correct position.
- The class then looks at the different pictures from each group and decides which group has drawn the picture that is closest to the one the teacher created.
- The science village or place can be created using any area of the science curriculum – for example, The Car Racing Circuit (Electricity) with Wire Bend, Crocodile Clip Corner, Battery Turning.

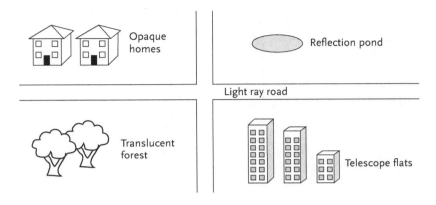

Figure 3 The science village – how good is your memory?

I SPY

Observation
Use and apply knowledge and understanding

Resources
None required

No book of games would be complete without a version of this old favourite. A great favourite with children, it is very easy to translate into science sessions, simply by explaining that whatever they spy must have something to do with science. Tell them that they can spy lots of different things, but show them that sometimes there can be a number of ways to give the clue, for example:

I spy a plastic animal beginning with D (duck).

I spy a resource beginning with M (magnets).

I spy a material that has a property beginning with W (children give the answer as a material that is waterproof e.g. plastic).

I spy equipment beginning with P (pipette).

I spy something beginning with C (condensation).

- For a more challenging game of I Spy you could tell the children that they might not be able to actually *see* the things! For example:

I am thinking of something you cannot see beginning with A (air).

I am thinking of something you cannot see beginning with L (lungs).

MYSTERY OBJECT

Observation
Analysis

Resources
Photographs of scientific objects taken from an unusual angle

This activity requires a bank of photographs. The pictures could either be taken by the teacher or by the children. However, once the collection has been created it can be used repeatedly, either with the same class (children love returning to activities) or with other children in the school.

- The photographs could be used as a slide show and quiz on the interactive whiteboard, the children having to guess the object. Alternatively, the photographs could be printed out and laminated for children to use at their table.
- When choosing objects to photograph think about

different aspects of science that would benefit from children having to analyse a picture. For example:

- pictures of parts of a plant, e.g. roots, stem, leaves, flower, ovary, anther;
- photographs of different scientific equipment such as beakers, magnets, thermometers;
- photographs related to an area of science, e.g. electrical appliances;
- photographs of different materials, e.g. wood, brick, glass, plastic;
- photographs of different parts of the body, e.g. elbow, nose, eye, ear, toes.

- Remember to allow children to return to the photographs; they love to repeat games and activities that they are familiar with. You could place the photographs on a science activity table for children to use.

CHAPTER 4
Jumpstarting science analysis

To analyse or carry out an analysis of something is an important part of scientific thinking and working. When we analyse something we can break it down into smaller parts so that we are better able to understand it. For example, we can analyse a problem, some data or an observation. In analysing something in more detail, we may find out more, thereby developing further our understanding in an aspect of science. Analysis also aids decision-making and drawing conclusions.

In this chapter the focus of the activities is challenging children to break down a question, a problem or a challenge so that it is easier to understand. Providing these kinds of experiences for children is important, particularly in helping them to make sense of data. Fun activities and games can motivate children to use and develop this area of their thinking.

One important aspect of the activities in this chapter is the need for children to be able to think and share their ideas, so discussion is central to learning. Childen should be able to articulate their ideas, challenge ideas held by others and use evidence to justify their decisions.

PLUS, MINUS, INTERESTING

Analysis
Decision making
Speaking and listening

Resources
Plus, minus and interesting scenario cards

This game is used to develop children's ability to make decisions by considering the pros and cons of a situation. It is a tool that helps children to think through whether or not something is appropriate by examining different aspects of a situation. It is excellent for helping them to think about alternative approaches, viewpoints etc. in science.

- PMI stands for Plus, Minus and Interesting.
- Children are given a statement or scenario and have to consider the Pluses, the Minuses and the Interesting, and place record their responses in a table.
- In the 'Plus' column children write down what would be positive about taking a particular action. Underneath 'Minus', the children would write any negative effects, and in the 'Interesting' column the children write down what they think might happen if they took that particular action.
- For example, children could be given the scenario that says that every house must have 'chocolate door handles'. Their task is to decide what the pluses are of having door handles made from chocolate, what might be the minuses and why it might be interesting.
- The children record their ideas in a table, for example:

Key stage 1

Table 2 PMI table. What if all door handles were made from chocolate?

PLUS	MINUS	INTERESTING
It would be great if you like chocolate – you would always be licking your fingers.	When the room was warm the handles would melt and you would not be able to get into or out of the room.	Chocolate manufacturers would get a lot of business because people would have to keep buying new door handles.

- There are many scenarios that the teacher could offer children linked to science. Here is one where the children are asked to consider, 'What if the force of gravity was less on Earth than it is now?' Their response might be:

Key stage 2

Table 3 PMI table. What if gravitational force on Earth was less than it is now?

PLUS	MINUS	INTERESTING
We would be able to move around by floating, so it would be easier because we could avoid crowds.	It might be very slow and we might not have control over our movements.	We might have to have floating lanes and traffic lights in the sky so people did not bump into each other.

The scenarios are endless, some very topical and others very imaginative:

- What if the climate where we live became very hot and dry?

- What if we did not recycle waste?
- What if we had eyes on our finger tips?
- What if we had microscopic robots in our bloodstream?

VOTE ON THE SOLUTION

Analysis
Decision making

Resources
None required

This activity focuses on children's ability to analyse a problem and then consider three or four different solutions. The children choose one solution from a given problem and explain their decision.

Allow children to work in pairs or small groups, on problems such as:

Teddy needs new sunglasses. How will we find out which material makes the best lens? (Key stage 1 or Lower Junior).

The town park gardens are being overrun by snails but the gardener can only use eco-friendly approaches to getting rid of them. How would you find out which is the best way? (Key stage 2 Upper Junior).

Once the children have thought about how to solve these problems, they share their ideas, which are logged on a whiteboard. In their groups children discuss each idea, the advantages and disadvantages (or they could use PMIs on page 35) and vote on which solution the class would use.

Of course, at this point the children might be able to use that solution as the basis for practical activity.

CAUSE-AND-EFFECT MAPS

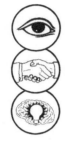

Analysis
Use and apply knowledge and understanding
Decision making

Resources
Large sheets of paper
Different-coloured pens

This activity introduces children to 'cause and effect maps'. These are used to help children think about ideas and what might be the causes of a specific problem or event. Children discuss the problem and think of a range of possibilities, rather than just one or two, or the ones that are the most obvious.

- Start the activity by giving children a large sheet of paper and different-coloured pens. Share the problem with the children. This might be the same problem to the whole class or different problems to different groups.
- The children write the problem in the centre of the sheet of paper and then each time they think of a possible cause they create a thinking bubble radiating from the centre. For example, children might be given the following statement:

In the town of Shenley there is a river that runs through the middle of the town. Residents have noticed that there are dead fish floating on the surface of the water and lying on the river banks. What do you think could have caused this?

- Encourage children to include all of their ideas and do not 'censor' what each person in the group says, so that all contributions are valued.
- When children have completed their cause-and-effect map, allow them to read maps created by other groups and leave comments. Encourage children to make positive comments based on the thinking and ideas that the group has shared on their map.
- Display the maps and allow children to add to their maps if they think of other ideas.
- This activity can also be used to encourage children to share their ideas when asked to plan a scientific fair test investigation.
- Cause-and-effect maps can be used to support children thinking through problems relating to specific areas of scientific understanding, for example:

The local council will not be able to afford to grit roads this winter. What do you think will be the effect of this decision?

Over the next 50 years, summers where you live will change and there will be more rainfall and less sunshine.

FACTS AND OPINIONS

Analysis
Decision making

Resources
Sets of fact statements or cards
Sets of opinion statements or cards

In science children need to develop an understanding of whether something is a fact or an opinion. This means that children need to analyse the statement, take it apart and be able to give reasons for their decision. This game aims to develop children's ability to distinguish between the two.

- Explain to children that facts are statements that can be proved.
- The river Thames is 346 kilometres (215 miles) long. That is a fact and it can be checked, just as the fact that the boiling point of water is 100°C can also be checked by using a thermometer.
- However, 'Everyone must recycle all rubbish in their home' is an opinion, and some people will agree with it and others will disagree. So is the statement, 'You should never eat sweets'; but the statement, 'Looking directly at the Sun can damage your eyes' is a fact.
- In this activity children create their own 'Fact' and 'Opinion' statements and share them with their science partner or the rest of the class, who then have to decide whether it is indeed a fact or an opinion.
- The challenging part of this activity is for children to create both types of statements. In doing so they have to understand the difference between the two and construct their own facts and opinion statements.
- Many children will find this activity easier if they can work with their science partner to create their statements and if they are able to draft and redraft them on their mini whiteboards.
- When the statements are completed on the mini whiteboards children can hold them up for the teacher and everyone else to read.
- They could then challenge the rest of the class to decide which of their statements is a fact or an opinion.

DATA HATS

Analysis
Data handling

Resources
Six data hats

This activity is based on de Bono's (2000), *Six Thinking Hats*, which are used to improve decision-making by wearing each one of the six thinking hats in turn. Here the six thinking hats have been changed to become six data hats to support children in developing their skills in analysing scientific data.

Figure 4 Data hats

- Adapting this technique to data-handling encourages children to think about different aspects of data-handling and develops their ability to understand and work with a variety of types of data. Suggestions for the different data hats are:

1. Black hat   Wearing this hat I look for PATTERNS in the data.

2. Grey hat   Wearing this hat I look for TRENDS in the data.

3. Spotted hat   Wearing this hat I look for ANOMALOUS READINGS in the data.

4. Star hat   Wearing this hat I look at the data and DRAW CONCLUSIONS.

5. White hat   Wearing this hat I CHECK THE GRAPH to make sure it is drawn correctly.

6. Striped hat   Wearing this hat I think about other questions that we could ASK and NEW QUESTIONS TO INVESTIGATE.

- When using the data hats children could either analyse data from their own science investigations or be given data produced by someone else.
- Using the data hats helps children to break down the different elements of data-handling and focus on one aspect at a time. Each child can support others in the group, helping to make decisions about the data.
- Alternatively, children can work on data as individuals or pairs and 'imagine' the data hat they are wearing or use 'Mini Card Data Hats' to help them work systematically through data. Some children will find it helpful if the data hats are also numbered so that they work sequentially through the data hats and the task.

WHAT WILL IT LOOK LIKE?

Analysis
Data handling

Resources
Selection of incomplete and completed graphs

Data-handling can be difficult for many children, so the more opportunities children are given to handle a range of data in different ways the more confident they will become. This type of activity should be used with children on a regular basis so that they become familiar with handling and analysing data.

- 'What will it look like?' is the key question the teacher asks when children are given different data-handling activities.
- Children could be given an incomplete line graph and copy it on to their mini whiteboard, analyse the patterns and trend in the line graph so far, and then complete the rest of the line.
- Provide children with a completed table of results and ask them to analyse the results and draw what they think they would look like as a bar or line graph on their mini whiteboard.
- Give children a scenario and challenge them to analyse it and then suggest what the pattern of the graph might look like – for example, if a bowl of hot water was left in the classroom to cool.

In each case the children should be asked not only to draw a draft of the graph etc. on their mini whiteboard but they should also be expected to explain why they have drawn the graph that way.

DATA DICE

Analysis
Data handling

Resources
Large cube dice
Paper and pens
Data-handling hats

Interesting and fun activities to support children in data-handling in science are few and far between. Here is a great activity for developing and extending children's ability to handle data. For this activity use large cube dice on to which can be placed sets of data, e.g. a completed table, line graph, bar graph, scatter graph or pie chart, depending on the ability of the children.

Some science or maths resource catalogues (e.g. TTS) produce dice with pockets on each face in which graphs and tables can be placed.

- When working in groups one child throws the dice.
- When the dice stops rolling the children look at the uppermost face and carry out the data-handling activity shown – for example, it might show a graph and the challenge is 'Tell the story of the graph' or 'Here is the graph, draw the table.'
- Alternatively when the dice lands the children use the 'Data Handling Hats' (see page 41) to answer questions about the data on the face of the dice. Using the hats means that a small group of children can work collaboratively on this activity.
- When they have completed those questions the children start over again and throw the dice. Children might wear one hat for a few turns and then swap their hat for another, so that they have a turn at wearing and using thinking in the style of each hat.

Figure 5 Data-handling cube

Dice can be purchased from TTS http://www.tts-group.co.uk

I PREFER . . .

Analysis
Decision making
Use and apply knowledge and understanding

Resources
None required

This is a quick game in which children are given some statements, ideas or information which they have to analyse and decide which one they prefer, but they must give their reasons for their choice.

- For example, the children could be given a list of foods such as chocolate, celery, pineapple, nuts or chips, then asked which one they would prefer to eat as part of a healthy diet. They might answer, 'I would prefer to eat pineapple because it contains lots of Vitamin C and can be eaten as part of my 'five-a-day'.

- The children can use a negative – for example, 'I would prefer not to eat nuts, because I am allergic to them'.
- Children might be given a list of possible solutions to a problem or different ways of carrying out a fair test investigation to answer a question. They would have to consider and analyse the different approaches and make sure that they give reasons for their final choice.

CHAPTER 5

Jumpstarting researching science information

In this chapter activities have been chosen that are firm favourites with children. Children are challenged to become 'mini experts' through researching information and sharing it with their classmates.

Firstly, for children to research something they need a question, even if it is, 'What do I want to know about . . .?' Then children need to decide how they are going to find the answer. For example, should they look in a book, on the internet, use a video, leaflet, poster, or ask someone. An important aspect of research is being organized and systematic. This requires someone to be focused and not waylaid by material that is of no consequence to the original question or problem. Once the information has been gathered the children will need to organize the information and decide how to communicate what they have found out, so they must know or consider their audience. Finally, when they answer their original question or other questions, they need to be concise and use appropriate scientific language.

There are so many layers of skills and understandings for children to develop when researching information in science that they need as many opportunities as we can offer them to become successful in this aspect of research.

SCIENCE TRIVIA GAME

Research information
Use and apply knowledge and understanding

Resources
Internet
Books e.g. *Guinness Book of Records*
Posters

This activity is designed to encourage children to access and make sense of information within a limited timescale and then share it with other children.

- Working in pairs or small groups, children are given a limited period of time to research as many facts as they can about something – for example, an animal such as a spider or a planet in the solar system. Allow children access to a range of books, posters, leaflets and internet sites (preferably which have already been located for them) to research their subject.
- Where children have appropriate writing skills they should jot down key facts as a list or they could create a mind map or use other ways to display their information.
- At the end of the time allocation they swap their information with another group. If the children were researching the same subject, they could collect additional information from other groups to add to their own facts.
- This activity is easily transferred to different areas of science and can be used to research facts about, for example, the heart, an unusual plant such as a Venus flytrap or a scientist.

HOT SEAT EXPERTS

Research
Use and apply knowledge and understanding
Speaking and listening

Resources
None required

This is a variation of the previous activity 'Hot Seating' (page 7). Unlike many of the other activities this is not a game but an activity that can be carried out with children working individually, in pairs or groups. In this version children become 'experts' in an area of science.

Children could choose or be given a topic to research. They should be given time to carry out their research and allowed to make notes etc.

- Children research a topic so that they become 'mini experts'. For example, children might research one of the planets, an invertebrate, a discovery, an invention or a famous scientist.
- The children then sit on the 'hot seat/s' – which could be seats decorated to make them 'special' – and answer questions asked by the audience.
- To help children remember information, teach them how to create their own 'prompt cards' using small index cards on which they can put key points to prompt them to remember key points.
- When the children have finished their time in the 'hot seat' they should be congratulated on being such brilliant experts.
- Remember to take photographs of children or video the 'hot seat' session.

SHARE A FACT

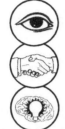

Research
Memory

Resources
Fact cards
Space in the classroom, hall or school grounds

This is a quick and fun way to introduce children to a range of facts about a specific aspect of science, such as bacteria or parts of the body.

- For this activity you will need to create a set of fact cards on a specific aspect of science. For example, you could use information from an internet site on bacteria to find relevant facts to make bacteria fact cards such as these:

  Bacteria come in all shapes: balls, spirals, cubes, rods; some are even shaped like the commas we use in punctuation.

  Bacteria are amazing. They can live in temperatures higher than boiling point and in cold that would freeze your blood.

  Each square centimetre of your skin contains about 100,000 bacteria.

  Some bacteria move using long, whip-like tails called flagella. They rotate (spin) their flagella like motors to propel themselves through liquid.

  Some bacteria move by oozing a slimy layer over surfaces, like slugs.

  You will need to make enough cards for each child in your class; it does not matter if some of the statements are repeated.

- Each child is given a fact card and told that they have to:
  - read their card;
  - memorize the information;
  - find someone else with a different card;
  - swap their cards;
  - read and memorize the information on the new card and go and find another new fact card to memorize.
- This is repeated until the time is up and the children go back to their groups and share the information they have remembered by writing facts on a large sheet of paper.
- When the children have completed sharing their information, ask them to review it and decide which is the most interesting fact.
- This can be applied to lots of other areas of science including:
  - functions of parts of the body;
  - animal adaptations; or
  - famous scientists.
- Finally, ask the children to visit the work of other groups, read what they have written and leave positive comments on their sheet of paper. For example:

  'Great, you remembered lots of facts.'

  'You remembered three things that we didn't. Well done!'

CHAPTER 6

Jumpstarting science communication

The games and activities in this chapter have been chosen to give children opportunities to communicate their science in interesting ways that link closely with approaches taught in literacy.

Most of the activities rely on children working together, sharing ideas and drafting and redrafting their writing. In all of the activities the teacher should challenge the children to use the correct scientific vocabulary, where appropriate.

ALPHABET CLUE

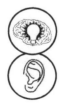

Communicating
Speaking and listening
Analysis
Scientific vocabulary

Resources
None required

The alphabet clue game works very well for challenging children to listen and think about the information given to them.

- When playing this game, the teacher gives the children a letter of the alphabet and a clue. For example:

The **I** *am thinking about does not allow electricity to pass through very easily.* Answer – Insulator

The **C** *I am thinking of is when water vapour cools and changes back into a liquid in clouds.* Answer – Condensation

The **S** *I am thinking about is the Earth's main light source.* Answer – Sun

The **F** *I am thinking about is a scientist who discovered penicillin.* Answer – Fleming

- As with all games the teacher can include a competitive element by dividing the class into teams and the teams can, if they wish, confer before they answer.
- Eventually children will become familiar with the game and become independent from the teacher.
- This activity can also be used with words related to scientific enquiry, as in the examples below.

The **V** *I am thinking about are things you can change in an investigation.* Answer – Variables

The **P** *I am thinking about is what we look for in data.* Answer – Pattern

The **G** *I am thinking about is what we can draw using our results.* Answer – Graph

The **D** *I am thinking about helps to show how we did our test.* Answer – Diagram

POSTCARDS FROM A HABITAT

Communicating
Use and apply knowledge and understanding

Resources
Blank postcards
A4 photocopies of blank postcards
Optional – copy of *Meerkat Mail* by Emily Gravett

Habitats are great topics and there are many quick games and activities which challenge children to use and apply their knowledge and understanding in creative ways about them.

- In this activity children will need to know the purpose and format of holiday postcards. This might require children to be given postcards to look at and practise writing messages. Work can be drafted on their mini whiteboards.
- *Meerkat Mail* by Gravett, E. (2007) is an excellent book that tells the story of a meerkat that travels the world and sends postcards back to the family from different places. However, on many of the postcards the meerkat indicates the reason why he does not like where he is, often because the habitat does not suit him.
- When children engage in this activity the teacher gives, or asks them to choose, a specific animal; it could be anything from a woodlouse to a shark. The children have to imagine that their animal has visited a certain habitat – for example, the woodlouse might visit the desert. The children draw a picture on the postcard of the woodlouse in the desert, and on the back of the card they write what they think of the habitat. The woodlouse might write:

Hi Everyone.

Just arrived in the desert. Very hot here, no shade and it is very dry. Not sure that I want to spend too long here. Looking forward to some rain and munching on some dead wood.

Bye
Woody Louse

- Make sure that when the children write their cards they are scientifically correct and the children use their knowledge and understanding. They could research information that they can use on their postcards.
- The different postcards could be placed in envelopes and displayed in a class big book called *Postcards from Animal Travels*, or if in the genre of *Meerkat Mail*, the big book could be called *Animal Mail*.

QUICK POEM

Communicating
Use and apply knowledge and understanding

Resources
Poem questions

Writing science poems is great fun but it can also be quite daunting. This is a good activity for children to try towards the end of a topic. It is very simple to do, but is best modelled with a whole class first before children work either individually or with their science partner.

- The children are given the questions below and answer them using only single words or phrases. It is important that children realize that they do not have to answer using complete sentences and also this is not a poem that has to rhyme.

What am I?	A butterfly
What colour?	Reds, blue, green and yellows
What shape?	Symmetrical
Where do I live?	On flowers
What do I eat?	Nectar
How do I move?	Flapping and floating
What do I remind you of?	A fairy in the wind

- Once the poem has been created ask the children to read it aloud. You and the children will be amazed how good it sounds.
- This approach to poetry in science is very effective and can be used for different aspects of science and with children from age 6 onwards. The questions above can be used with living things, but changing the questions can allow poems to be written about other aspects of science. For example:

What am I?	Electricity
What do I do?	Light the world
Where can I be found?	In pylons and wires
What do I remind you of?	A caged animal ready to charge

SCIENCE WORD POEMS

Communicating
Use and apply knowledge and understanding
Scientific vocabulary
Revision

Resources
Key scientific words

This activity offers another opportunity to link science with literacy and create a poem using key scientific vocabulary connected with verbs.

- The teacher gives children key words in science (nouns) and asks them to add a word to describe what it does with the ending '-ing'.
- The children must use a word that explains the function of the noun, as in the examples below.

Flower attracting	**Battery** charging
Petal enticing	**Wires** conducting
Stamen producing pollen	**Filament** glowing
Pollen fertilizing	**Bulb** lighting
Ovary containing eggs	**Circuit** working
Seed germinating	

- This is an activity that is more appropriate towards the end of a topic when children have developed their understanding of key scientific words. Other topics that work well with this activity are:

Magnetism   Light   Life cycles   Water cycle   Forces

SCIENCE NURSERY RYHME

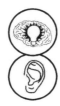

Communicating
Use and apply knowledge and understanding

Resources
Copies of nursery rhymes

Writing poems in science is an excellent way to develop science understanding creatively. This activity is a fun way to create science poems using existing nursery rhymes and it teaches children how to change the rhymes using what they know from their current topic.

- Children find this activity much easier if the teacher models with the whole class how to change nursery rhymes and update them.
- Place the original nursery rhyme on one side of the whiteboard or flip chart. Then, line by line, change the words with ideas from what children have learned recently in science.
- Once the children have been involved as a whole class, allow them to create their own, working in pairs or groups of three.
- Give children the opportunity to share what they have created, then give each group another nursery rhyme to change.

Becomes

Mary, Mary, quite contrary	Mary, Mary, quite contrary
How does your garden grow?	How do your cabbages grow?
With silver bells	With stripey snails
And cockle shells	And slimy slugs
And pretty maids all in a row.	And butterfly eggs in a row.

NEWSPAPER HEADLINES

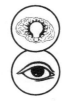

Communication

Resources
Newspaper articles

This activity makes clear links with literacy in developing children's ability to write in a precise and concise way using newspaper headlines.

- When children have completed a science fair test investigation, take them through analysing their data and drawing conclusions. (You could use the Data Hats activity, page 41.)
- Make sure that they understand the nature and purpose of newspaper headlines; that is, headlines
  – summarise an article;
  – are short and eye-catching;
  – can be humorous; and
  – encourage the reader to want to know more.
- It is better if the children work in small groups or with their science partner to create their newspaper headline based on the science fair test investigation they have just completed and, in particular, their conclusion.
- Encourage children to use their mini whiteboards to draft and redraft their newspaper headline. They might offer more than one suggestion. Provide time for children to share their ideas with the rest of the class and, where appropriate, children could write up their science fair test investigation in the form of a newspaper article using the headline that they have created.
- Examples of children's headlines for the investigation 'Which sugar dissolves the fastest?' are:

FASTER CASTOR
CASTOR DISAPPEARS FROM VIEW

- The children could make headline posters for a classroom display.

TEXT IT!

Communication

Resources
Mobile phone

Have some fun with this activity where the children, particularly upper primary, communicate their science using a mobile phone.

- Start off by telling the children to draw a mobile phone on their mini whiteboard.
- Then give the children a statement, and ask them to translate it into a text message and write it on their mini whiteboard. For example:

> Make sure that you update your science
> word book before Friday.

As a text message it would look something like:

> Mk sure u upd8 yr sc wrd bk b4 Fri

- Then, give children a text message to change back. For example:

> Nxt time u do a fr tst, chk ur grf,
> does it hv lbls, axis and tle.

Translated it says:

> Next time you do a fair test, check your graph.
> Does it have labels, axis and title?

- There is a very good reason for doing this. Besides children having fun, it makes them think carefully about what they are writing. In particular, it is very useful when children are asked to draw a conclusion and write it as a text message because it challenges children to be concise and to think carefully about the sentence construction.
- You could put text messages about science on the interactive whiteboard; they could be questions to start off a lesson or activity, or something for the children to puzzle over whilst waiting for other children to clear up.

CHAPTER 7
Jumpstarting science revision

The activities in this chapter have been put together to help children revise what they know, whether it is at the beginning or end of a lesson, topic or year. Fun activities can help children use and apply knowledge and understanding and skills in science. Some of the activities help children to develop personal study aids such as using mnemonics to remember concepts and information. All these activities challenge children to use and apply their knowledge and understanding in science.

TALK BALL

Use and apply knowledge and understanding
Science vocabulary

Resources
This activity uses what is called a 'talk ball' which can either be purchased from a science catalogue or made using an inflatable beach ball. Using Blu-Tack, stick words or questions on to the ball.

Children really like this game, in which they

Figure 6 Talk ball

Image: TTS Group

have to throw the talk ball to someone in the classroom and the recipient has to do whatever is asked of them in the question that is underneath one of their hands.

- The challenge and complexity of the task will depend on the age and ability of the children and what the teacher decides should be the focus of this game. For this reason the teacher creates the challenges and sticks them on to the ball. Make sure that they are firmly attached so that they do not fall off when the ball is thrown or caught. Examples of challenges could include:
  - a question to answer, e.g. 'Why do plants need roots?'
  - a forfeit – for example, 'Melt like a piece of ice', 'Grow like a seed', 'Mime day and night with a friend'.
  - word(s) to define, e.g. evaporate.
- When the child has completed the task they can then throw the talk ball to someone else in the classroom.
- A variation on this activity is where children stand in a circle and the ball is passed round. When the music stops whoever is holding the ball has to ask one of the questions of someone else in the circle. Once the question is answered correctly the game continues.
- A slightly different version is where the music is substituted for the following chant.

> The question ball goes round and round
> To pass it quickly you are bound
> If you're the one to hold it last
> The question is yours then to your friend pass!

Talk balls can be purchased from TTS http://www.tts-group.co.uk/

SHARE IT

Use and apply knowledge and understanding
Speaking and listening

Resources
Large sheets of paper for each group
Different-coloured pens for each group

This activity sees the children having to think about and share knowledge and understanding in science.

- In this activity children could work in groups of four to six.
- There are a number of ways that this activity can be used. The first is based on each group sharing what they know about one topic. Each group has a large sheet of paper on which they write what they have learned about a topic. All of the children can offer something, either individually or through a group scribe. They must all use the same colour pen and must not repeat anything that is already on the page.
- After a set time all the groups complete the statement they are writing and then move on to the next table. As they move around the tables children get a chance to see what others have written. They can then add something to the work on that table, but they should do so in the correct colour pen for their own group. This helps to distinguish the contributions from different groups.
- The same rules apply when the children write on the next table's work. Everyone can contribute but they cannot repeat what is already on the page. Children might add something that they have written on another table, or the content of the new sheet might prompt children to remember something different and offer a new contribution.
- The activity ends when the groups are back to their original tables.

If this activity is played towards the end of a school year then an alternative approach could be for each of the sheets on the table to cover the topics from each term and the children to remember things about each of the different topics and add them to the sheet.

I KNOW A FACT

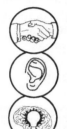

Use and apply knowledge and understanding
Speaking and listening

Resources
Large beach ball or sponge ball

This is a quick and fun activity to play. It is very easy to carry out yet it demands children's full attention and participation.

- The idea is that a soft ball is thrown randomly from one child to another around the classroom. Whoever catches the ball has to make a statement telling everyone else something that they know about a given area of science – for example, how a plant lives, electricity, floating and sinking.
- The challenge is for children to remember what others have said, because they are not allowed to repeat any fact or piece of knowledge. If they do, they have to sit out.
- This could be used at the beginning of a topic to find out what children already know or at the end of a topic. Alternatively, it could be used as a revision activity.
- This is a great way to help children develop their ability to take turns, speak clearly and concisely in science and use appropriate scientific vocabulary.

SILLY MATERIALS

 Use and apply knowledge and understanding

Resources
None required

When teaching the topic Materials, children are usually asked to name objects made of specific materials. This is relatively straightforward and not particularly challenging for most children, whereas this game *is* challenging and the responses can be very funny.

- In this activity children are challenged to apply their knowledge and understanding of materials and their properties in a more creative way. Instead of asking for appropriate applications of different materials the teacher asks children to think of inappropriate uses.
- For example, give the children a material such as concrete and ask children to think of inappropriate uses for the material, the sillier the suggestion the better. You will be surprised what children suggest. For example, concrete shoes, concrete pillow and a concrete life jacket are just some suggestions children give.
- Ask children to think about inappropriate uses for materials such as:
  - chocolate;
  - newspaper;
  - glass;
  - marshmallows;
  - wood;
  - metal;
  - concrete.
- Of course this game has a serious side since it challenges children to apply their understanding to unusual applications, which is more challenging than asking for suggestions of everyday objects.

- Collect children's suggestions in a class book called *Silly Materials* and encourage them to keep adding to this book.

OPPOSITES

Use and apply knowledge and understanding
Scientific vocabulary

Resources
None required

This is a quick activity, which is great when teaching science topics such as Materials and their properties.

- It should be played as a quick-fire activity where the teacher or a child calls out a word and the children have to suggest an opposite – for example:

Conductor – Insulator	Push – Pull
Transparent – Opaque	Predator – Prey
Rigid – Flexible	Solid – Liquid
Rough – Smooth	Evaporation – Condensation

- An alternative approach to playing this game is to give children a set of scientific word cards, so that children can play the game in pairs. If they play this as a group game then one person should be the caller who asks each child in turn to give an opposite.
- For some children it might be easier to make pairs of cards, and they have to find matching pairs.

TRUE OR FALSE

 Use and apply knowledge and understanding

Resources
Sets of statements

The object of this game is for children to be able to use subject knowledge and understanding and reasoning skills to decide which of a series of statements are true and which ones are false.

- Give children a series of statement cards and ask them to sort them into two sets, 'True' and 'False'.
- It is much easier if each group is given a different set(s) of cards printed on different-coloured paper or card, so that if the sets are accidentally mixed up they can be easily sorted.
- An example of a set of cards on plants is given below, along with the answers.

    1. The heaviest apple was grown in Hirosaki City, Japan. It weighed 1.849 kg (4 lb 1 oz). (T)
    2. Plants eat soil to help them grow. (F)
    3. A banana has no water in it. (F: it is about 75% water).
    4. The hurricane plant has holes in its leaves that keep it from being destroyed by wind. (T)
    5. Seeds have a protective outer layer called the seed coat. (T)
    6. Flowers are important in making seeds. (T)
    7. Some plants, but not all, have flowers. (T)
    8. Roots help to hold the plant up and take water from the soil. (T)
    9. Some trees are believed to be over four-thousand years old. (T)
    10. A plant bulb can be used to light a room. (F)

- Once children have played their set of cards they can swap with another group to try a different set of cards.
- Children could create their own 'True of False' cards for others to play.
- Don't forget to leave the cards out on a Science Activity Table for children to use in their own time.

SCIENCE RIDDLES – WHAT AM I?

Use and apply knowledge and understanding

Resources
None required

Children love solving and creating riddles and this activity will be a firm favourite with children in science lessons.

- Start off by modelling some science-based riddles so that children understand how they are written. For example:

  I live in the garden
  Gardeners do not like me
  I eat lots of plants
  I only have one foot
  I carry my home on my back
  What am I?

  I have six sides
  I am transparent and translucent
  I am below 0°c
  Leave me out and I will change state
  What am I?

- Once children know how to write riddles then they can begin to make their own and then share them with other children to see if they can guess the answer.

- Some riddles are based on rhyme, and a great way to link science with literacy is to teach children how to offer the first line of a riddle and then how to respond using rhyme. The idea is that children listen to the first line and then they have to make up their own second line, but it does have to fit with the first line. It does not matter if the response is not what the first person was thinking about, as long as it works. Here are some examples:

This is a word which rhymes with a boat you can row.
It is found on the end of your foot because it is a toe!

I'm useful for measuring temperature.
I have lots of numbers on me because
I am a thermometer.

You can find me near ponds and won't catch me even if you try.
That's because I move very fast and I am a dragonfly.

- As with any activity of this kind the key issue is to challenge children to use their science knowledge and understanding and correct scientific language.

DARTBOARD QUESTIONS

Use and apply knowledge and understanding
Speaking and listening

Resources
Magnetic or inflatable dartboard

Figure 7 Inflatable dartboard

Inflatable dartboards can be purchased from TTS http://www.tts-group.co.uk

Children love this game, which is played almost exactly like a game of darts but with a science twist. The magnetic dartboard can be easily purchased, or you might find that there is one in school that is being used for mathematics.

- Divide the class into teams.
- At the beginning of the game each team nominates someone to throw one dart and the team with their dart nearest to the bullseye gets to choose the topic for the questions – for example, children could choose from any of the following:
  - forces;
  - creating circuits;
  - animals;
  - the human body;
  - habitats;
  - materials and their properties.
- The members of each team take it in turns to throw a dart when their team is at the dartboard. When the magnetic dart hits the board, the children in the team have to answer a question correctly in order to win the points. The whole team can collaborate

to answer their science question. If they answer correctly, then, as in the real game of darts, the number is deducted from 501 (or a lower number).

- The first team to reach zero wins. Unlike the real game of darts children do not have to finish on a specific number. As long as the dart thrown takes the score to zero or below, the team wins.

DEM BONES

Use and apply knowledge and understanding

Resources
A selection of large and small dog biscuits shaped like bones

This activity is great fun and can be used across the age ranges. It focuses on children learning parts of the body and animal skeletons using a collection of 'dog bones'. It can be used:
- to find out what children know about skeletons before and after a lesson;
- as a revision activity; or
- as an observation activity.

- You will need a collection of dog biscuits, including large and tiny biscuits that children will use to make skeletons. Round dog biscuits work well as a head and for joints. Keep the dog biscuits in plastic containers or bags and be warned that they can smell a bit, but this wears off as the activity progresses.
- Give the children a selection of dog biscuits and, working with 'science talk partners', ask the children to talk about the different dog bones and how they can use them to make their skeleton. Begin by challenging children to make a human skeleton, and offer a range of support – for example, tell them to feel the bones in their own

body or give children models or pictures of the human skeleton.

- The great thing about this activity is that once children have made their skeleton they can jumble the dog bones and start again. They could then focus on one part of the body such as the skeleton of a hand or a foot.
- This activity can be extended by giving children body part labels to place alongside different bones. Alternatively, ask children to make their own labels and captions that explain the function of some bones and joints.
- Children can also make animal skeletons. There are lots of animal skeleton x-ray pictures on the internet, and the book *Funnybones* by Ahlberg, A. and Ahlberg, J. (1999) offers great support for this activity.
- This activity can be made into a game by challenging the children to make animal skeletons for others to 'guess the animal'.
- Don't forget to take digital photographs of the skeletons as a record of what the children have been doing. You could put the different pictures in a class book called *Our Book of Skeletons*. Alternatively, if you don't mind using up the bones, children could make a skeleton to take home by gluing the bones on to a piece of card.
- Leave the bones out on a science activity table for children to return to and make their own skeletons.

INSIDE A FOOD WEB

Use and apply knowledge and understanding
Scientific language

Resources
Food web cards – photographs of animals, sun, plants and arrows
Space in the classroom, hall or school grounds

This game requires one set of large food web cards for the whole class or smaller sets of cards so that children can play this game in groups of five or six.

- The aim of the game is to create a food chain (or a more complicated food web) using the cards. Each child is given part of a food chain and they have to place themselves in the correct position in the chain.
- To add to the element of fun the children could be placed into teams and the first team to organize themselves on to the correct version of the food chain gains a point.

For example:

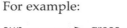

sun ———→ grass ———→ rabbit ———→ fox

sun ——→ nettle ——→ snail ——→ thrush

- When creating the food web cards ensure that you make arrow cards as well because these are an essential part of a food web. Ensure that children place the arrows in the correct direction, always showing the route from the original producer to the final consumer.
- Of course, children could create their own food web cards. The teacher checks them and then children swap their sets and have to put together a food web created by other children in the class.
- Take photographs of children in their food chains as evidence of the activity and children's attainment.

SORT THE CYCLE

Use and apply knowledge and understanding
Speaking and listening

Resources
Pictures of a cycle, e.g. life cycle, water cycle

In this activity children are given a set of cards on which there are pictures (or words) relating to a cycle in science – for example, the life cycle of a plant or animal, or the water cycle.

* The cards are mixed up and the children have to discuss and make decisions about the correct order, giving their reasons for the sequence they have chosen. The discussion element of this activity is important, since one aim is for children to justify their choices. For this reason, the activity works best when it is played by pairs or small groups of children.

A variation of this game is to provide children with the cards to sequence but to leave one of the cards out, and the children have to decide what in the sequence is missing. When they have made that decision, challenge them to create their own card to replace the one that is missing. Ask them to think about what part of the sequence it should show and ask them to draw the card.

SCAVENGER HUNT

Use and apply knowledge and understanding

Resources
Science related objects
Science related words

This is a team-based activity where pairs of children or larger groups are sent on a scavenger hunt for objects that can be found around the classroom, school building or school grounds.

- The children are given objects to search for in a given area linked to the current science topic or as revision for a previous topic.
- For example, if the topic is electricity the children could be asked to find ten objects that are made from materials that are electrical conductors, or insulators.
- Alternatively, children might be engaged in an activity that revises an aspect of science such as materials and their properties. The teacher could ask children to find objects that are opaque, translucent or transparent and an added challenge could be that children have to return with the objects and place them into the correct set labelled 'transparent', 'translucent' or 'opaque'.
- When the time is up, allow children to check the objects collected by another group and decide whether they are appropriate. Children could give points for each correct item.
- Children could collect objects that are made from materials that are:
  - magnetic or non-magnetic;
  - thermal insulators;
  - different invertebrates from the school grounds;
  - plastic animals hidden around the classroom or school grounds relating to animal groups, e.g. mammals, birds, reptiles, insects.

JUST 30 SECONDS

Use and apply knowledge and understanding

Resources
Vocabulary cards or word mats
Stop watches, stop clocks or interactive whiteboard clock

This activity is most appropriate played towards the end of a topic since it relies on children being able to talk about an aspect of learning.

- The activity can be played in number of ways – for example, it could be played as a whole class where children work in pairs. They are given a word – for example 'plant', and between them have to talk about the word, say, for 30 seconds without taking a pause. If one child stops the other child in the pair can continue to make sure that the flow of talk is not broken.
- The end of the time is indicated by a 'fun sound' like a klaxon.
- An alternative approach would be to give pairs a stop watch and a set of word cards. The deck of word cards is kept in the centre. One person turns over a card, reads it and then the other person starts the timer. The first person has to talk about the word on the card, without pausing, for 30 seconds. The children keep score and swap over to let the other person have their turn.

SIMON SAYS

Use and apply knowledge and understanding

Resources
None required

This is another great favourite with children and a game that is easily translated into science. It is brilliant for helping children to learn or revise parts or functions of the body.

- One person is chosen to be Simon, who calls out an action for the children to follow.
- In its simplest form, Simon tells the children to touch different parts of the body – for example, with very young children, 'Simon says touch your nose'. As their knowledge and understanding of body parts increases, commands could include:

'Simon says touch your knee cap.'

'Simon says touch your patella.'

'Simon says touch where the organ that pumps blood is found.'

- If any of the children get the action wrong then they have to sit down. The last person who is standing can then be the new 'Simon'.

MNEMONICS

Use and apply knowledge and understanding

Resources
None required

Mnemonics are an easy way for children to recall certain information. One of the most common mnemonics in science is MRS GREN, which is a way of helping children to remember the activities of living things; **M**ovement; **R**espiration; **S**ensitivity; **G**rowth; **R**eproduction; **E**xcretion; **N**utrition.

When developing mnemonics with children, keep it simple and focus on those aspects of learning that require children to know a number of associated words – for example:

The planets of the solar system

Parts of plant

Order of colours of the rainbow

Children could use mnemonics to help them remember the elements of a fair test investigation, for example: plan, observe, measure, record, analyse and conclude.

- When children have created their mnemonics, ask them to make a mini poster so that it can be displayed and shared with the rest of the class.
- Ask children to think about aspects of science that they find hard to remember and challenge them to create a mnemonic to help them remember them in future.

References

Ahlberg, A. and Ahlberg J. (1999) *Funnybones*. London: Picture Puffin.

De Bono, E. (2000) *Six Thinking Hats*. London: Penguin.

Gravett, E. (2007) *Meerkat Mail*. London: Pan Macmillan.

Jumpstart!

Drama

Games and Activities for Ages 5–11

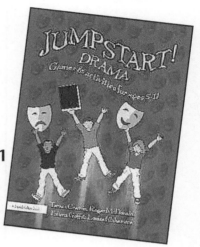

Teresa Cremin, Roger McDonald, Emma Goff and **Louise Blakemore**

There are more than forty engaging drama activities in this book to 'jumpstart' the reading, writing and sharing of drama in every Key Stage 1 and 2 classroom. Practical, easy-to-do and highly motivating, the drama 'jumpstarts' will appeal to busy primary teachers who wish to enliven their practice and make more use of drama. Whilst the examples will connect to English texts, theconventions can be used in a variety of subjects, and will suit avariety of learning styles.

Jumpstart! Drama will enable teachers to learn to use literary and non-fiction texts in a dramatic and motivating manner.

March 2009
Pb: 978-0-415-48248-6: £11.99